A Smart Kid's Guide to Personal Finance



# How to Manage Risk

Ryan Randolph

PowerKiDS press

New York

Published in 2014 by The Rosen Publishing Group, Inc.
29 East 21st Street, New York, NY 10010



First Edition

Editor: Jennifer Way
Book Design: Greg Tucker

Photo Credits: Cover Stan Honda/AFP/Getty Images; pp. 4–5 Rose Hayes/Shutterstock.com; p. 6 Elena Elisseeva/Shutterstock.com; p. 7 Ernest R. Prim/Shutterstock.com; p. 8 Alexander Raths/Shutterstock.com; p. 9 Jerry Sharp/Shutterstock.com; p. 10 Serder Tibet/Shutterstock.com; p. 11 (top) digitaldarrell/Shutterstock.com; p. 11 (bottom) Lisa S./Shutterstock.com; pp. 12–13 © iStockphoto.com/Eliza Snow; p. 14 Christopher Edwin Nuzzaco/Shutterstock.com; p. 15 Brand X Pictures/Thinkstock; p. 16 JGI/Jamie Grill/Blend Images/Getty Images; pp. 17 (top), 22 kurhan/Shutterstock.com; p. 17 (bottom) Jack Hollingsworth/Brand X Pictures/Getty Images; pp. 18–19 Blend Images/Ariel Skelley/The Agency Collection/Getty Images; p. 20 Comstock/Thinkstock; p. 21 Jose Luis Pelaez Inc/Blend Images/Getty Images.

Library of Congress Cataloging-in-Publication Data

Randolph, Ryan P.
How to manage risk / by Ryan Randolph. — First edition.
pages cm. — (A smart kid's guide to personal finance)
Includes index.
ISBN 978-1-4777-0745-6 (library binding) — ISBN 978-1-4777-0831-6 (pbk.) —
ISBN 978-1-4777-0832-3 (6-pack)
1. Finance, Personal—Juvenile literature. 2. Risk management—Juvenile literature. I. Title.
HG179.R3236294 2014
368—dc23

2012045384

Manufactured in the United States of America

CPSIA Compliance Information: Batch #S13PK5: For Further Information contact Rosen Publishing, New York, New York at 1-800-237-9932

# Contents

# What Is Risk?

Has a teacher ever told you to be more careful? He was trying to keep you out of danger. He was trying to reduce your **risk**, or the chance that you would get hurt.

There are other kinds of risks, too. Drivers can get into car **accidents**. Houses can be damaged by fire. These things are not only upsetting, but they can also hurt people **financially**. The term "risk management" means "the things people do to plan for **emergencies**." These can be things that make you safer, as well as things that protect you from financial losses. This book will explain some of the things people do to manage risk.

Skateboarding is an activity in which there is a high risk of injury. People wear helmets to reduce the risk that they will be badly injured if they fall.

# Risky Business

Wearing a life vest when on a boat is an example of being safe and prepared.

If a parent loses her job, there is a risk her family will not be able to pay bills. If a fire damages a family's house, there is a risk they will not have enough money to pay for the repairs.

The first step in managing risk is being safe and prepared. It is smart to have emergency savings that can be used in case of a job loss or unexpected expenses. Good fire safety practices can prevent house fires. Accidents still happen, though. After doing your best to prevent accidents, the next part of risk management is **insurance**.

People have insurance to protect their homes from fires and storms, but they also make emergency plans to keep themselves safe and prepared for emergencies.

# What Is Insurance?

An insurance agent explains different types of policies to her clients. She wants to make sure they understand what is covered and what is not.

Being safe and prepared is not always enough to manage risk smartly. People can buy insurance to help manage risk. Insurance is part of financial planning. This means that insurance helps people plan for the money needs they may have in the future.

People have insurance to protect things that cost a lot of money. Insurance costs a little money each month. If something bad happens, insurance helps pay for the thing that costs a lot of money. An **insurance policy** is an explanation of what things the insurance company will cover. For example, a car insurance policy shows what is covered if something happens to a car.

When there is a house fire, insurance helps people repair their home or find a new home as well as replace the things they lost.

# Health and Life Insurance

Health insurance helps pay for regular doctor and dentist checkups as well as visits for sicknesses or emergencies.

Insurance is not just for things that cost a lot of money. People buy health insurance for themselves and their families. Nobody knows when he will get sick or hurt. Doctors and hospitals cost a lot of money. That is a lot of risk. This is why people buy health insurance.

Life insurance can help a family financially if a parent dies. It may help pay the expenses of a funeral.

In a family, parents earn money at their jobs. There is a risk that a parent could die. This is sad. It also means the person earning money is no longer there. People buy life insurance to manage the risk of a parent or loved one dying.

Disability insurance policies help people when they cannot work due to sickness or injury. People might choose to have this in addition to health insurance.

# Insurance Basics

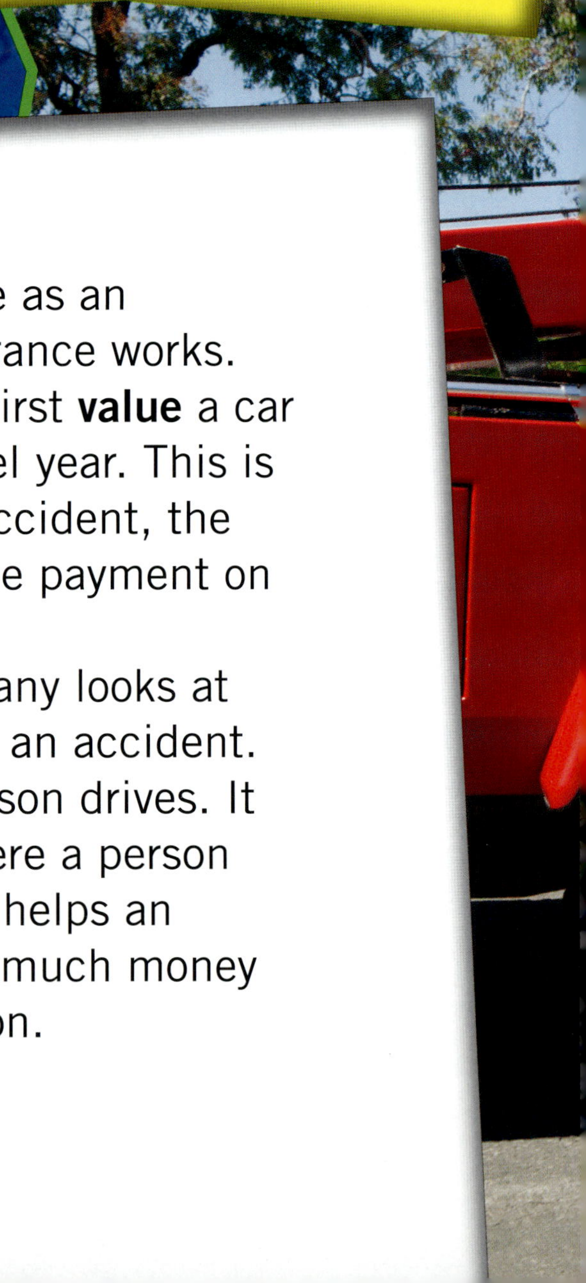

Let's look at car insurance as an example of how having insurance works. An insurance company will first **value** a car based on its make and model year. This is because if the car is in an accident, the insurance company bases the payment on the insured car's worth.

Then the insurance company looks at the driver's risk of getting in an accident. It will look at how well a person drives. It will also look at age and where a person lives. All of this information helps an insurance company set how much money insurance will cost the person.

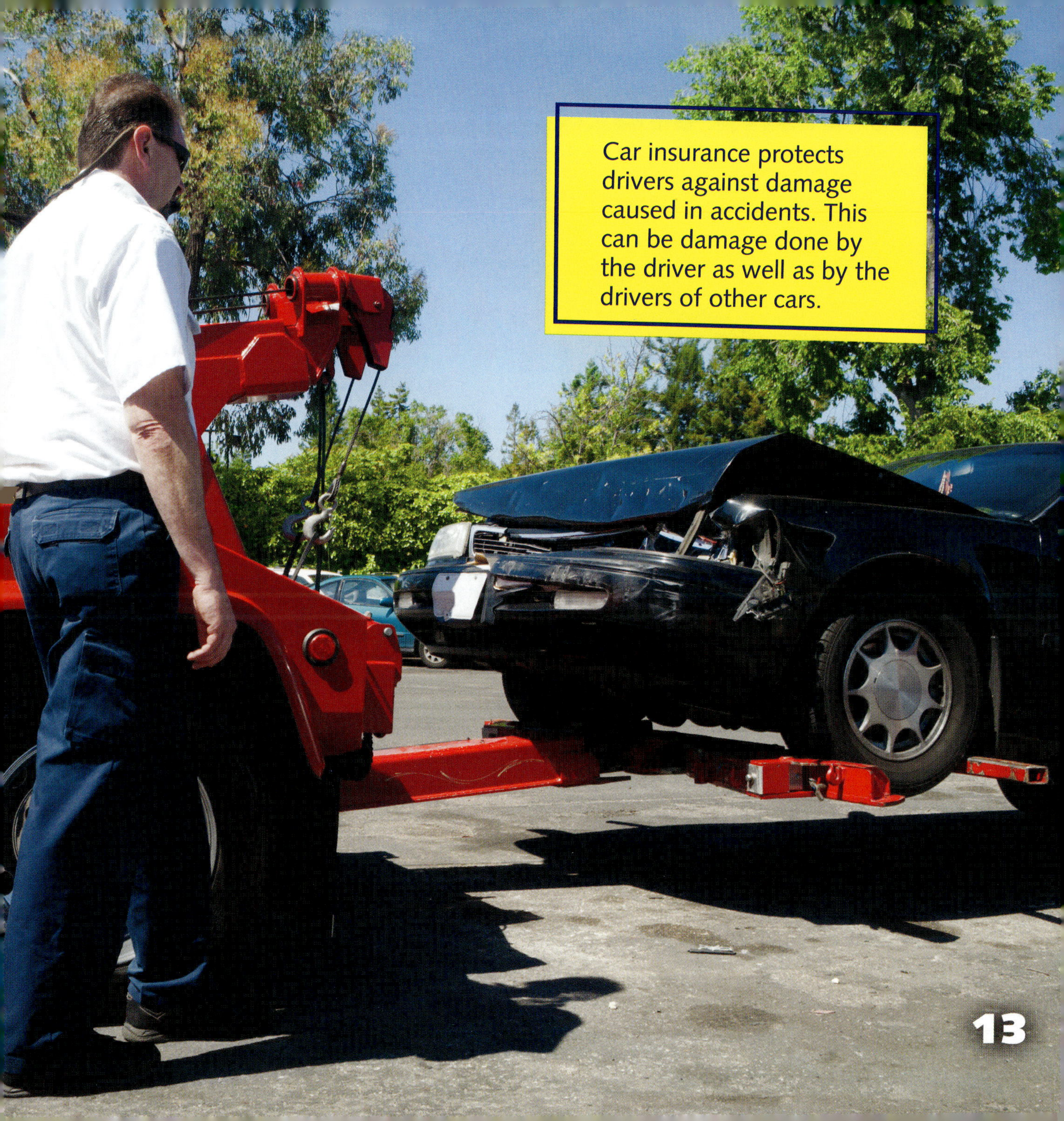

Car insurance protects drivers against damage caused in accidents. This can be damage done by the driver as well as by the drivers of other cars.

# How Wills Work

When a person makes a will, she decides things like to whom her house will go. Having something willed to you is called inheriting.

When people die, they may have money, a house, or other **assets**. No one wants to think about death or what should happen after he dies. Having a plan for what happens after one's death is another part of financial planning and managing risk.

Many people make a will when they start a family. That is because they want to decide who would look after their children if they die.

A **will** is a financial plan for what happens to money and property when a person dies. A will can also be used to name who takes care of the children if their parents die. If a person dies without a will, the laws of the state she lived in determine these things instead. Having a will protects against the risk of this happening.

# Using Savings to Manage Risk

Having savings is another way that people manage risk. Savings do not replace the need for insurance, but they make hard times less difficult.

For example, a person who keeps a rainy-day fund for emergencies is better prepared for when things happen, like a washing machine needing repairs.

People may need to rely on their savings while they look for a job. Their savings help manage the risk of not being able to pay their bills when they have no income.

It is smart to have a rainy-day fund for unexpected expenses, like home repairs.

It is easier on a person's **budget** if that unexpected expense can be paid for from her savings. Many people even have a goal of building up an emergency savings equal to several months of their income. They do this to protect against the risk of losing a job and being unable to find work right away.

While a person is paying her bills, she might choose this time to set aside money into her savings. This helps her add to her savings regularly.

# Finding Out More About Risk

Luckily there are good resources to help find information on insurance and managing risk. Many people use an insurance agent to help them find the right insurance coverage. When it comes to investing and saving, many people use a financial planner. For wills, lawyers help people put these plans in place.

Of course, all of these people who help cost money. Some people prefer to do it themselves. For those who do, there are many books and websites that show people how. Many resources are also available for kids! A teacher or librarian can help guide students to good sources.

A financial planner helps people figure out how they can best manage financial risks in their lives. He might tell them things they should talk to a lawyer or insurance agent about.

# Responsible Risk Management

**Financial responsibility** means being smart with money. There are financial consequences to not managing risk. Most people do not have enough savings to pay the big cost of hospital bills or repairs after an accident. This is why insurance is important.

Managing risk protects people from large, unexpected expenses. The smaller, regular expense of insurance gives that protection as well as peace of mind.

In many places, car insurance is even required by law. Health insurance can also be required by law.

When it comes to managing risks, saving money and buying insurance are not the only things that matter. Being prepared and staying safe go a long way to preventing accidents. They are also part of thinking of the future and being smart with money.

People can receive tickets or fines for not having car insurance. In some cases, a person might have her driver's license taken away for a period of time.

# Smart Risk Management Tips

1. Insurance costs money. Being smart with money also means being a good shopper. When shopping for insurance, looking for the right amount of insurance for the lowest price is important.
2. There are a few ways to pay less for car insurance. Having a safe driving record lowers car insurance payments. For young drivers, getting good grades in school can help, too.
3. There are also ways to pay less for life insurance. Being in good health and not smoking can lower the cost of life insurance.
4. A **warranty** is a type of insurance in case something breaks. Companies offer warranties on things like TVs and computers. You have to decide whether a warranty is worth the cost.
5. When it comes to investing, there are lots of different risks. Bonds and stocks both carry a risk of losing money. Understanding the risk of different investments is important.

# Glossary

**accidents** (AK-seh-dents) Unexpected and sometimes bad things that happen.

**assets** (A-sets) People's property.

**budget** (BUH-jit) A plan to spend a certain amount of money in a period of time.

**emergencies** (ih-MUR-jin-seez) Events that happen in which quick help is needed.

**financially** (fuh-NANT-shu-lee) In a way that has to do with money.

**financial responsibility** (fuh-NANT-shul rih-spont-suh-BIH-luh-tee) Using money wisely and well.

**insurance** (in-SHUR-ints) Protection against loss or harm.

**insurance policy** (in-SHUR-ints PO-luh-see) An explanation of what the insurance company will pay for.

**risk** (RISK) The chance that one could suffer harm or loss.

**value** (VAL-yoo) To put an amount on something that people agree it is worth.

**warranty** (WAHR-un-tee) A type of insurance that covers the replacement of a product if it breaks.

**will** (WIL) A legal document describing how a person's property will be handled after that person's death.

# Index



# Websites

Due to the changing nature of Internet links, PowerKids Press has developed an online list of websites related to the subject of this book. This site is updated regularly. Please use this link to access the list:
www.powerkidslinks.com/skgpf/risk/